Grammar

in use

Intermediate

WORKBOOK

with answers

THIRD
EDITION

William R. Smalzer
with Raymond Murphy

CAMBRIDGE
UNIVERSITY PRESS

CAMBRIDGE UNIVERSITY PRESS
Cambridge, New York, Melbourne, Madrid, Cape Town, Singapore,
São Paulo, Delhi, Dubai, Tokyo, Mexico City

Cambridge University Press
32 Avenue of the Americas, New York, NY 10013–2473, USA

www.cambridge.org
Information on this title: www.cambridge.org/9780521734783

First published 1989
Third Edition 2009
5th printing 2011

Printed in Hong Kong, China, by Golden Cup Printing Company Limited

A catalog record for this publication is available from the British Library.

Library of Congress Cataloging in Publication data available

ISBN 978-0-521-73477-6 Student's Book with answers and CD-ROM
ISBN 978-0-521-73476-9 Student's Book with answers
ISBN 978-0-521-75936-6 Student's Book with CD-ROM
ISBN 978-0-521-73478-3 Workbook with answers
ISBN 978-0-521-73479-0 Workbook

Art direction, book design, layout services, and photo research: Adventure House, NYC

Contents

To the Student

Grammar in Use Intermediate Third Edition Workbook provides you with additional practice in North American English grammar, building on the grammar points presented and practiced in the *Grammar in Use Intermediate* student's book. It offers additional exercises on difficult grammar points and a variety of exercise types. The workbook will be useful in helping you apply what you have already learned in the student's book.

The workbook covers the same grammar points as the student's book and in the same order. The types of exercises in the workbook are often different from those in the student's book, however. This way you can apply what you have learned in a slightly different way. The exercises in this workbook will also help you understand how the grammar points in one unit of the student's book are related to the grammar in other units. You may be called on to use several different grammar structures in one exercise.

In general, workbook exercises will require you to read longer passages and write longer responses than the exercises in the student's book. In some exercises, you will rewrite whole sentences using different grammar forms but keeping the same meaning. In other exercises, you will read paragraphs and fill in blanks with correct forms, or answer questions that call on your understanding of grammar. In personalized review exercises, you will have the chance to use your own ideas to write sentences or short paragraphs.

Level

Like the student's book, the *Grammar in Use Intermediate Third Edition Workbook* is intended mainly for intermediate students (students who have already studied the basic grammar of English). The workbook is not suitable for beginning learners. However, advanced learners who have problems with grammar will also find the book useful.

How the workbook is organized

There are 170 exercises covering all 142 units in the student's book. One exercise in the workbook may cover the grammar in one unit or more than one unit in the student's book. Each workbook exercise has a heading that indicates the unit(s) of the student's book covered in that exercise.

Workbook exercises are grouped into sections, according to the sections in the student's book (see the Contents). There are periodic personalized review exercises that cover several or all of the units in a section. These allow you to practice using the grammar in the units to express your own personal ideas.

How to use the workbook

Use the workbook only after you have completed the corresponding units in the student's book. If you have trouble with the exercises on the right-hand pages of the student's book, review the left-hand pages of those units. Then do the workbook exercises for those units.

Checking your work

After you have done an exercise or group of exercises in the workbook, check your answers in the Answer Key at the back of the book. You can use the Answer Key in several different ways:

Students working alone

Check your answers at the back of the book.

Students working in pairs

Student A: Read your answers to Student B, who will tell you if they are correct.

Student B: Refer to the Answer Key as you listen to Student A answer each item. In case of errors, try to help your partner find the correct solution rather than just reading it.

Groups of four or more (working in pairs)

Work with a partner on an exercise. Decide on your answers together. When you finish, compare answers with another pair of students. Discuss any differences. Finally, check the Answer Key together.

Groups of four or more (working with a leader)

Choose a leader. The leader opens the book to the Answer Key. The other group members take turns reading their answers. For each answer, group members compare their own solutions to the one they heard, discussing any differences. The leader, after listening to all the other members, reads the correct response.

If you do not understand an answer in the Answer Key, ask your teacher or someone who knows English well to explain the answer to you. The personalized review exercises that ask you to use your own ideas often don't have sample answers in the Answer Key. For these exercises, the Answer Key says, "Answers will vary." If possible, check your answers for these exercises with someone who speaks English well. If you are studying in a class, your teacher may check your answers to those exercises.

To the Teacher

Grammar in Use Intermediate Third Edition Workbook provides exercises to reinforce and extend the grammar presented and practiced in the *Grammar in Use Intermediate* student's book. An exercise in the workbook often covers more than one unit in the student's book in order to help students consolidate their knowledge of different grammar points. Thus, workbook exercises are often slightly more challenging than exercises in the student's book, in addition to having more varied formats.

The workbook covers all 142 units in the student's book. At the beginning of every workbook exercise is a heading which indicates the title(s) and number(s) of the relevant unit(s) in the student's book. Intended to supplement the student's book, workbook exercises should be done after the relevant units in the student's book have been completed. Exercises in the workbook are organized into sections, corresponding to the sections in the Contents in the *Grammar in Use Intermediate* student's book. Personalized review exercises occur regularly, after every 10 exercises on average, to help students move from very controlled exercises to ones where they give freer responses using the grammar in question.

This book will be most useful for students at the intermediate and upper-intermediate levels. It will also be useful for more advanced students who need further practice on particular grammar points. It is not suitable for students at the beginning or low-intermediate levels. Like the student's book, the workbook can be used by whole classes, by individual students needing extra help, or for independent study. Many of the exercises lend themselves better to writing than to oral work. These exercises may be done independently, or by students working together in the classroom.

This edition of the workbook contains an answer key. Exercises that ask students to use their own ideas do not usually have sample answers because there will be such a wide variation in student responses. Students are encouraged instead to check their answers with someone who speaks English well. You might want to look over student answers to these exercises or have students compare answers in groups. An edition of the workbook without an answer key is also available.

What's New?

- Ten new exercises on phrasal verbs have been added to practice the nine new phrasal verb units in the *Grammar in Use Intermediate Third Edition* student's book.

- Many of the exercises from the previous edition have been revised or replaced to give more complete coverage of the points in the student's book. The number of items in many exercises has also been increased to provide students with more practice.

- There are now more exercises in which students work with paragraph-level texts. These are either stories or dialogs in which students complete the blanks with the correct tense of the verb, an adverb, a phrasal verb, and so on.

- There are now more personalized review exercises. These exercises give students strong guidance for using the grammar from several units at once as they write sentences or whole paragraphs about their own lives and opinions. These exercises generally occur at the end of each section, but they may also appear midway through longer sections. Many are new; older ones have been modified to make it easier for students to get started with the task.

- Five appealing art-based exercises have been added in which students find visual information that helps them describe events and conditions by using the correct grammar.